Celebrating
the Seasons
with Children

To our children
Jill Elizabeth
and
Timothy Gordon

Celebrating the Seasons with Children

*Conversation Ideas
Based on the Common Lectionary
Year B*

PHILIP E. JOHNSON

THE PILGRIM PRESS
New York

Second printing, 1988

Unless otherwise noted, the biblical quotations in this book are from
the *Revised Standard Version of the Bible,* copyright 1946, 1952, and
© 1971, 1973 by the Division of Christian Education, National
Council of Churches, and are used with permission. In some cases the
quotations have been adapted for inclusive-language purposes. The
excerpt from the *Good News Bible,* the Today's English Version of the
New Testament is copyright © 1966, 1971, 1976 by the
American Bible Society.

Library of Congress Cataloging in Publication Data

Johnson, Philip E., 1943–
Celebrating the seasons with children.

Includes indexes.
1. Children's sermons—Outlines.
2. Bible—Homiletical use.   I. Title.
BV4315.J624   1984   251'.02   84-14791
ISBN 0-8298-0723-3 (pbk.)

The Pilgrim Press, 132 West 31 Street, New York, NY 10001

CONTENTS

ACKNOWLEDGMENTS

Special thanks to:

All children with whom I have shared precious moments especially in worship.

The ministers of Maple Grove United Church, Oakville, Ontario, Canada, whose pastor I am and whose journey of faith I am privileged to share.

Joy Lawrence, my friend in Christ, who has prepared my manuscript with love and excellence.

David Peacock, my friend, whose creative spirit inspires and delights through art.

Lyn, my wife, who by her love, patience, encouragement, and gracious presence makes every day a celebration.

INTRODUCTION

Celebrating the Seasons with Children provides pastors, church school teachers, and other group leaders with a collection of tested, stimulative ideas for conversations with children aged four to eight in the context of Christian worship or other Christian educational settings.

The ideas emerge from the biblical readings for Year B of the *Common Lectionary* and therefore follow the flow and emphasis of the seasons of the liturgical year. With the exception of the season of Pentecost, for which the readings do not have a thematic unity, I have developed a theme common to the readings for the day and have suggested a title, resources, and a prayer. These conversations can also be used by those who are following *An Inclusive Language Lectionary,* Year B, and, of course, by those who follow no lectionary.

Persons who tell the Christian story are affirmed and encouraged to integrate their own faith, imagination, and creativity in their own particular situation. Children are also affirmed and encouraged to appropriate a sense of the story of God's interaction with humankind as their own story. In addition, they are invited to experience the richness of God's grace now through the faithful personhood of and interaction with the storyteller.

Planning well in advance is important. I have found it advantageous to plan about a year ahead in order to coordinate my conversations with the lectionary readings and with events in the life of the congregation, such as anniversary Sunday or the annual stewardship campaign. This resource will assist you as a catalyst in the planning process. My suggestions are not to be followed slavishly, but are to be a springboard for your own faithful creativity. For example, when the object referred to is unavailable, a picture of the object or another object can be substituted. Choose objects that help communicate your message.

Exercise care if you are having a conversation with children in the context of worship. A children's hymn during which the children gather at the front can effectively draw them together without "putting them on display" and can indicate to them that they indeed have a special place in the Christian community. I sit down with the children at the front and wear a microphone because I discovered a long time ago that adults are influenced profoundly by what is said to the children. Also be careful to ensure that whatever is said or done is appropriate to worship and that each child is attended to in the spirit of Christ. The greatest gift a storyteller can give is the gift of his or her presence.

To celebrate means to keep or to remember. This book is intended truly to celebrate the seasons of the church year with children!

The Season of Advent

Christmas Is Coming!

Lesson 1: Isaiah 63:16—64:8
Lesson 2: 1 Corinthians 1:3–9
Gospel: Mark 13:32–37

Theme: Advent is a time to prepare for the celebration of Christmas.

Resource: An advent wreath: a circular wreath covered with greenery (usually evergreens) in which four candles (three purple and one rose) are placed. A larger, more substantial white candle is placed in the center of the wreath as the Christ candle.

Development: Advent literally means coming. It is a time for renewing our expectations and hopes for life as we prepare for the "coming" of Jesus. Soon children will enthusiastically be getting ready for Jesus' birthday by making their own Christmas wish list and by being involved with family preparations, including shopping, baking, and decorating. Some may be rehearsing for a Christmas pageant.

To heighten their awareness of this season, read them the Gospel lesson with emphasis on watching, getting ready, and being alert. Let the story content speak for itself. Then offer the advent wreath as a way to help them get ready for the best Christmas celebration ever! Explain that the four candles remind us of Jesus, the light of the world, and represent the four weeks of Advent. The first and second lessons focus on waiting, and you may want to indicate that four weeks seems like a long time to wait. Invite a child to light the first purple candle.

Prayer: Dear God, help us to get ready for your coming. Amen.

ADVENT 2

Hear Ye! Hear Ye!

Lesson 1: Isaiah 40:1–11
Lesson 2: 2 Peter 3:8–15a
Gospel: Mark 1:1–8

Theme: Advent is a time for repentance and forgiveness.

Resources: Advent wreath; trumpet; megaphone (or strong voice); town crier's hat

Development: The preparation for the Sovereign's coming continues with the emphasis this Sunday on repentance and forgiveness. Isaiah's words of encouragement to the people in exile in Babylonia—words that aroused their hopes and dreams—are quoted by Mark as a prelude to John the baptizer's preaching of "a baptism of repentance for the forgiveness of sins [Mark 1:4]," indispensable ingredients for the celebration of Christmas. John, who baptizes with water, announces that the One is coming who will baptize with the Holy Spirit. The lessons all announce good news and invite repentance and forgiveness.

Sound the trumpet and read the Gospel in the style of a town crier (the hat is good visually): Hear ye! Hear ye! "The beginning of the gospel of Jesus Christ. . . ." Encourage the children to get ready for Christmas by repenting and assure them of God's forgiveness.

The second lesson provides an understandable analogy for repentance: Be spotless or get cleaned up! Point out that purple is the color of the advent season and of repentance, and light the first and second purple candles of the advent wreath.

Prayer: Thank you, God, for your forgiveness. I want to get cleaned up for Christmas. Amen.

Christmas Countdown!

Lesson 1: Isaiah 61:1–4, 8–11
Lesson 2: 1 Thessalonians 5:16–24
Gospel: John 1:6–8, 19–28

Theme: Advent is a time of anticipation.
Resources: Advent wreath (scented rose-colored candle); model space rocket; video or audio soundtrack of a countdown

Development: The focus in the lessons today is joy. Isaiah "greatly rejoices" in God who has anointed him and given him everything he needs to "bring good tidings to the afflicted." There is almost a launching that occurs in verse 11: "God will cause righteousness and praise to spring forth before all the nations." Paul encourages the church at Thessalonica to "rejoice always," and John, in the Gospel, notes the joy that will come with the Light.

Advent joy is the joy of anticipation and is different from mid-Lent joy, which is like refuge in the wilderness, and from Easter joy, which is born of sorrow. Advent joy expresses expectations and looks forward with faith to Christmas Day. Begin by asking the children, "Can you wait until Christmas?" Chat with them about their wishes and hopes and dreams for Christmas, or generally. Share their anticipation and compare it with an astronaut's feelings during countdown. A model rocket will direct their attention. Actually count down with them, using a countdown tape, if possible, and stop at "two" to mark the two weeks of Advent until Christmas liftoff. You may want to have a minicountdown to Christmas (without going into orbit) when you light the advent wreath candles: two purple and one rose. Pink is the color of joy.

Prayer: Dear God, we're really looking forward to Christmas! Amen.

ADVENT 4

For You!

Lesson 1:   2 Samuel 7:8–16
Lesson 2:   Romans 16:25–27
Gospel: Luke 1:26–38

Theme: Advent is a time to receive God's love.
Resources: Advent wreath; Christmas card in envelope for each child

Development: The fourth Sunday in Advent, the final stage in preparation for Christmas, centers on God's love. Point out that the advent wreath is in the shape of a circle, reminding us that God's love has no beginning and no end. Also point out that the evergreens symbolize the new life God gives us, especially the new life found in Jesus. Quietly, count down the weeks of Advent, letting the children recall their advent journey with the lighting of each of the four candles.

  The first lesson and the Gospel combine to demonstrate how we must be open to receive God's love. David's and Mary's openness to receive God's love made their greatness possible—David, to be ruler of the people of Israel, and Mary, to be the mother of the Child of God. Impress on the children that they are the ones God has chosen to offer the most gracious gift of all at Christmas. God gives. We may receive. Express your hope that each child may receive God's gift of love at Christmas, just as each may receive the

Christmas card you are going to give him or her. On the envelope, print "For You!" and write a greeting on the card. Your personal note will be a sign of God's love as well.

Prayer: Dear God, thank you for loving me and choosing me to receive your Child. Amen.

The Christmas Season

Love Light

Lesson 1: Isaiah 62:6–7, 10–12
Lesson 2: Titus 3:4–7
Gospel: Luke 2:8–20

Theme: Celebration of the birth of Jesus in Bethlehem
Resources: Advent wreath with Christ candle in the center; tapers tied with white ribbon for everyone

Development: Children get so excited about Christmas naturally. In such a marvelous condition they will be open to and receive more from an experience than a lot of linear content about Jesus' birth. Seize the opportunity to bring children and adults together to delight in the image of Jesus, the light of the world, developed during Advent, using the advent wreath. The Old Testament lesson sets the tone and reason for the celebration of light: "The people who walked in darkness have seen a great light; those who dwelt in a land of deep darkness, on them has light shined. . . . For to us a child is born [Isa. 9:2, 6]." "The good news of a great joy [Luke 2:10]" has finally come to all people in the birth of Jesus in Bethlehem.

After reading the Gospel invite the children to form a circle of love (the advent wreath shape) to receive the "love light" of the Christ candle. Give each person a taper tied with a white ribbon, signifying the gift of light to the world. Invite a child and an adult to light the Christ candle together, and then carry the candle around the circle so that each taper can be lit from the symbol of the Light. Use as few words as possible, and let the "love light" permeate the celebration. Tapers may be taken home and burned, for example, during Christmas dinner.

Prayer: O loving Light of the world, we thank you for the gift of Jesus. Amen.

Old Simeon

Lesson 1: Isaiah 61:10—62:3
Lesson 2: Galatians 4:4–7
Gospel: Luke 2:22–40

Theme: Simeon's affirmation that Jesus is the Holy Child
Resource: Simple costume to depict Simeon

Development: The first lesson states the promise that "God will cause righteousness and praise to spring forth before all the nations [Isa. 61:11]." Isaiah vows that he will not be silent until that day when Jerusalem has been vindicated and saved. The second lesson and the Gospel record the fulfillment of God's promise in the coming of God's Child. "When the time had fully come, God's Child was sent . . . to redeem . . . [Gal. 4:4–5]." Luke paints a moving picture of the identification of Jesus as God's Child by Simeon, a righteous and devout man, who longed to see Israel renewed.

Why not try a welcome change of pace today, after the flurry of Christmas activities? Instead of reading the Gospel, become Simeon—put a robe on and tell his story. Saturate yourself with his faithful character and the story line, and let Simeon's discovery come alive in you. If you feel a little uneasy about doing this, just remember that most of the children will probably be seeing Simeon for the first time. You may want to delegate this opportunity to be Simeon to someone else. Outline what you want to say, rehearse if necessary, and stay in character, even for the closing prayer.

Prayer: Gracious God, we thank you for sending your Child Jesus to save us all. Amen.

365 Gifts

Lesson 1: Jeremiah 31:7–14
Lesson 2: Ephesians 1:3–6, 15–18
Gospel: John 1:1–18

Theme: God's gift of time

Resources: A large calendar of the year ahead, tied with decorative ribbon; stickers to place on days of importance

Development: During the liturgical season of Christmas we celebrate our births in life, and today we remember the birth of a new year to be lived in Christ's presence. It is, of course, Jesus' birth that signals us to be born again every day of the year.

The first lesson and the Gospel combine to inform and inspire us about the meaning of time. "For everything there is a season, and a time for every matter under heaven: a time to be born, and a time to die," writes the author of Ecclesiastes [Eccles. 3:12]. He continues: "I know that there is nothing better for them than to be happy and enjoy themselves as long as they live [Eccles. 3:12]." Time is given to us, says Jesus in his teaching about the bridegroom, to be present to one another while we are actually with one another.

Show the calendar tied with ribbon, indicating that each day of the year ahead is a gift to us from God to live fully. We can work, play, sleep. We choose how we will use the 365 gifts of time God gives us to enjoy. Take the ribbon off the calendar and place stickers on days that are important to the children: birthdays, Easter, vacation, and so on. If there's time, you may want to talk about their favorite seasons.

Prayer: Dear God, thanks for giving me today and every day. Amen.

Epiphany and the Season Following

A Light in the Dark

Lesson 1: Isaiah 60:1–6
Lesson 2: Ephesians 3:1–12
Gospel: Matthew 2:1–12

Theme: God is revealed in Jesus Christ, the light of the world.
Resource: Flashlight

Development: Epiphany, from the Greek word meaning revelation, is the season that celebrates God's presence in the world through Jesus Christ. Although there is a perpetual epiphany, these few weeks focus on the themes of light, discipleship, baptism, and the mission of the church. Whereas Christmas is the celebration of the humanity of God, Epiphany is the celebration of the divinity in humankind.

Traditionally, the Feast of Epiphany—sometimes called Twelfth Night because it is observed twelve days after Christmas, on January 6—recalls the story of the wise men coming to bring gifts to the Christchild. This story is the Gospel for today and picks up the emphasis on light in the two lessons. Isaiah's familiar exhortation, "Arise, shine; for your light has come [Isa. 60:1]," and the light of wisdom in Ephesians combine to reinforce the image of Jesus as the guiding light. Just as a star led the wise men from the East to Jesus' birthplace, so Jesus is the one whose light leads us to the truth of God's unfolding love. In this season, Christ is officially recognized as prophet, priest, and sovereign.

A brief introduction connecting the idea of light in Advent and Christmas with today's image of Jesus lighting up our lives will provide a smooth transition from season to season and foster the rhythm of the church year. Tell a story of finding your way by seeing the light from your own experience, or relate how sailors look for the lighthouse to give them direction on the water, just as Jesus gives us direction in our lives. Use of the flashlight will make the story vivid for them.

Conclude by indicating that once we have seen the light of God's love, we can be God's light for others in the world today.

Prayer: Light of the world, light up my life. Amen.

EPIPHANY 1
(BAPTISM OF OUR SOVEREIGN)
A Bad Dream

Lesson 1: Genesis 1:1–5
Lesson 2: Acts 19:1–7
Gospel: Mark 1:4–11

Theme: The baptism of our Sovereign Jesus
Resource: Baptismal font

Development: The readings from Acts and Mark address the matter of baptism with water and baptism with the Spirit. John does the former, a baptism of repentance for the forgiveness of sins, and Jesus performs the latter. Note that Jesus, who is sinless, who really doesn't "qualify" for John's baptism with water, is indeed baptized by John in the Jordan. God obviously concurs with this action by saying, "You are my beloved child: with you I am well pleased [Mark 1:11]."

Let the baptism of Jesus speak to the children as the way in which God lets all of us know that we are part of the same family. Jesus is baptized just like us. Explain that Jesus wanted us to know for sure that God is always with us. The baptismal font can be used as an effective symbol to remind the children of God's presence from week to week.

Ask them to remember when they had a bad dream at night, called out for help, and a parent came and hugged them, saying that everything was all right because the parent was with them. Assure them that, in the same way, our loving God is always with us no matter what happens.

Prayer: Dear God, our Mother and Father, thanks for being with us always. We trust you. Amen.

EPIPHANY 2

Called by Name

Lesson 1: 1 Samuel 3:1–10
Lesson 2: 1 Corinthians 6:12–20
Gospel: John 1:35–42

Theme: God knows us and calls us by name.
Resource: Telephone book

Development: The importance of names is reflected in the first lesson and in the Gospel. In 1 Samuel, God calls, "Samuel! Samuel!" and the boy responds to his name and listens to God. In the Gospel, Simon is given a new name, Cephas (which means Peter, which in turn means rock), and a number of names are used to identify Jesus: Lamb of God, Rabbi, and Messiah.

Tell the story of how Simon had his name changed by Jesus, and then ask the children their names. Talk about how necessary names are to identify people, especially if you want to find their numbers in the telephone book. Leaf through the phone book, demonstrating that people and businesses and cities and schools and parks all have names. Point out that people usually have a family name and one or more Christian names, and that God knows and calls each of us by name.

You may want to add a word or two about the names we give to God, but a whole conversation could be set aside to do that. During Epiphany it is enough perhaps to realize that God calls us by name to carry the light of Christ to the world.

Prayer: O Creator, thank you for making me and calling me by name. Amen.

EPIPHANY 3

The Big Turnaround

Lesson 1: Jonah 3:1–5, 10
Lesson 2: 1 Corinthians 7:29–31
Gospel: Mark 1:14–20

Theme: Jesus calls us to repent and follow him.
Resource: U-turn sign

Development: Jesus began his ministry in Galilee preaching: "The time is fulfilled, and the [realm] of God is at hand; repent, and believe in the gospel [Mark 1:14]."

Ask the children what they think repent means. Explain that it means to change one's mind, to make a U turn (use sign), and that Jesus, in the Gospel lesson, was really inviting people to change their minds, to turn away from their sin and follow him.

Tell the story of the calling of the fishermen and how they repented and made the big turnaround— left their fishing nets and followed Jesus to "catch" or persuade other people to join them and follow Jesus too. Refer to the Old Testament reading, in which Jonah, after his big turnaround, preached to the people of Ninevah, who made the big turnaround by confessing their sins and believing in God. Indicate that God calls us by name (as we mentioned last week) to repent, to turn away from our sin, and follow Jesus. We are then called to go into the world to proclaim good news and call people into the realm of God.

Prayer: O God, I repent and believe and want to follow you. Amen.

EPIPHANY 4

A Great Teacher

Lesson 1: Deuteronomy 18:15–20
Lesson 2: 1 Corinthians 8:1–13
Gospel: Mark 1:21–28

Theme: The teaching ministry of Jesus
Resources: Chalkboard and chalk

Development: Let us focus today on the teaching ministry of Jesus, a ministry that the children can identify fairly easily because of their experiences in school and elsewhere. The Gospel describes Jesus as the one who taught with authority, not like the scribes, who in all likelihood were somewhat authoritarian. The reading from Deuteronomy adds a prophetic dimension to teaching in that the words put in the prophet's mouth have a divine origin. It is not knowledge as such, therefore, that gives Jesus' teaching authority, but rather divine inspiration. It is abundantly clear that Jesus' words have the power to heal, persuade, and encourage. Paul echoes the prophetic dimension when he says that "'knowledge' puffs up, but love builds up [1 Cor. 8:1]."

Ask the children to name all the qualities they think a great teacher possesses, and write these qualities on the chalkboard. You might suggest that they think about a great teacher they once had, now have, or would like to have and describe his or her qualities. Their insightful answers will help you to reveal Jesus as the greatest teacher of all. He listened, was patient, liked to have fun, knew what he was talking about. Jesus is our teacher who truly believes in us and, in the derivative sense of education (from *educo*, which means to lead out), leads us into all truth.

Prayer: Teach me, dear God, so I can be me. Amen.

EPIPHANY 5

All in One Piece

Lesson 1:   Job 7:1–7
Lesson 2:   1 Corinthians 9:16–23
Gospel: Mark 1:29–39

Theme: The healing ministry of Jesus—wholeness

Resource: A human puzzle: Trace on a large piece of fairly heavy paper, doubled, the outline of a child lying down, with legs and arms away from the body. Cut along outline, and then cut one shape into large puzzle pieces.

Development: The fourth through seventh Sundays of Epiphany treat various aspects of healing, with particular emphasis on the healing ministry of Jesus. Today's lessons combine to proclaim the healing power of Christ, who invites his hearers to seek wholeness.

In this context, note that wholeness and holy and health have a common origin.

In the Old Testament lesson, Job's predicament is highlighted with graphic images. Here is pictured a righteous man who has maintained his integrity and who is suffering from almost every conceivable domestic and economic calamity. He can't sleep. He has no hope. His flesh is covered with worms and dirt. He is the prime example of human misery. Mark's Gospel describes long days in the life of Jesus as he travels from town to town healing people with various diseases and casting out demons. Paul's dedication to using any means to bring people to an acceptance of the gospel is pointed out in the epistle lesson.

Focus on the theme of wholeness with the children, and invite them to place and tape the puzzle pieces on the full body outline cooperatively. While enjoying this activity, chat about the things we could do to be healthy or whole, things that keep our spirits and minds and bodies in shape for God. Tie this idea of responsibility for our health to the wonders of medical science, the mystery of healing, and our calling by God to reach out to the world with God's healing touch. When all the pieces are in place, turn the outline over and show the solid figure to indicate that God wants each person to be "all in one piece."

Prayer: Dear God, help me to grow all in one piece with you. Amen.

Bubbling Over!

Lesson 1: 2 Kings 5:1–14
Lesson 2: 1 Corinthians 9:24–27
Gospel: Mark 1:40–45

Theme: Two lepers are healed.

Resources: Photograph of a human body afflicted with leprosy; glass of water and a bubble-producing substance

Development: Both the first lesson and the Gospel deal with stories about lepers who wanted to be healed. In the Old Testament lesson, Naaman, the commander of the king of Syria, travels to the king of Israel and then to Elisha, God's person, to be told by the prophet to go down and wash himself seven times in the Jordan River. When he did as he was told, "his flesh was restored like the flesh of a little child, and he was clean [2 Kings 5:14]." The Gospel of Mark relates how a leper comes to Jesus to be healed. After he is cleansed, he "disobeys" Jesus by telling the good news of his clean condition.

Begin this Sunday by inviting the children to listen closely to a condensed, free-style telling of these two marvelous stories, and ask them to identify the disease the two sick men had. Inquire if they know what leprosy is, and share that, although leprosy in biblical times was considered the result of sin, it was really a skin disease. At this point it would be helpful to show a photograph or slide of a person with the disease. Then help the children feel through what it must have felt like for the leper to be healed and how he just had to tell the good news.

To demonstrate the latter image, put any bubble-producing substance in a glass of water. Ask the children to tell you about times when something really great has happened to them and perhaps how they could hardly wait to share the news. Confirm that God wants us to tell the good news of our Creator's healing power and that God heals people today just like they were healed long ago.

Prayer: Dear God, I'm bubbling over because of your love. Amen.

EPIPHANY 7

Erase

Lesson 1: Isaiah 43:18–25
Lesson 2: 2 Corinthians 1:18–22
Gospel: Mark 2:1–12

Theme: God heals and forgives.
Resource: A personal computer

Development: In today's readings the healing power of God brings wholeness through forgiveness and faithfulness. Isaiah points out that even though Yahweh is tired of Israel's empty religious observances and burdened with their sins, God vows to forgive their sins and bring the people back from exile through the wilderness. The same God revealed in Jesus Christ forgives the sins of the paralytic and heals him: "My son, your sins are forgiven. . . . I say to you, rise, take up your pallet and go home [Mark 2:5, 11]." Paul, in his epistle, reminds the church at Corinth that the God he serves is faithful in all things.

To formulate an adequate understanding of the graciousness of God, a child must be exposed to the reality of divine forgiveness. The Gospel story presents a picture of what happens when forgiveness is accepted: a paralytic gets up and walks away. Care must be taken to ensure that Jesus in this instance is not perceived as a kind of superstar TV faith healer.

Forgiveness, in God's scheme of things, is to truly forget our sin—really forget! Zero in on this point by using a personal computer. Enter something so that it is displayed on the screen. Demonstrate that when the erase key is pressed, what was on the screen is gone. It cannot be retrieved or remembered. If you have a printer, you could compare the two printouts: one with the entered material recorded and the other one blank. God's forgiveness, you must impress on the children, is essentially like that. God keeps no record or "memory" of our sins. We are forgiven by God and called to forgive others.

Prayer: Forgiving God, thank you for forgiving me. Amen.

EPIPHANY 8

Good Reflectors

Lesson 1: Hosea 2:14–20
Lesson 2: 2 Corinthians 3:1–6
Gospel: Mark 2:18–22

Theme: Jesus calls us to reflect God's love on the world.
Resources: Flashlight; mirror; globe

Development: The primary thrust of the second lesson and the Gospel is that when we belong to Christ or put on the "new" person, old religious ways are inappropriate and "new" ones need to be developed. Mark records how fasting, an established tradition practiced by John's disciples and the Pharisees, cannot possibly be observed while the "bridegroom" is still with them. Parabolically, "No one sews a piece of unshrunk cloth on an old garment . . . and no one puts new wine into old wineskins [Mark 2:21–22]." A new age has come in which we cannot be enslaved by the past and in which we must accept the new relationship with God and not be bound by the limitations of the old. A new covenant has been made. Paul speaks of the personal witness to the truth in the new covenant: "You yourselves are our letter of recommendation, written on your hearts, to be known and read by all people [2 Cor. 3:2]." We present Christ in our persons and so reflect God's glory.

Recall with the children how God has shined on us in Jesus, who is the Light of the world. Shine the flashlight, representing the Light, on each of them to personalize God's love. Then point out that God wants us, like a mirror, to reflect God's light on the world. Invite a child to hold the mirror so that the light from the flashlight reflects off the mirror onto the globe or other people present. Encourage the children to reflect God's love on the world today—to be good reflectors.

Prayer: Light of the world, keep shining on me. Help me to be a good reflector. Amen.

EPIPHANY 9

"Aha!"

Lesson 1:   2 Kings 2:1–12a
Lesson 2:   2 Corinthians 4:3–6
Gospel: Mark 9:2–9

Theme: The transfiguration of Jesus
Resources: Digital watch or microchip; lamp

Development: The season of Epiphany closes today with readings that once again extend the image of God's revelation in Jesus Christ as the Light that touches all humankind. The transfiguration of Jesus in the Gospel is preceded by the revealing encounter among God, Elisha, and Elijah in 2 Kings. Both passages reflect the mystery of "mountaintop" experiences in which God's presence is revealed by a transforming vision or dream. Assuredly, these stories are a mystery for our contemplation and not a logical set of data for our intellect to reason through. The transfiguration marks the turning point in the Gospel record. From here on, Jesus proceeds to his passion and death and the disciples see more clearly in whom it is they believe and how to live faithfully.

Before reading the Gospel, invite the children to be part of the "dream" story and to imagine that they are with Jesus and Peter and James and John on the high mountain. Read the story and share what you all felt. Explain that for the disciples it was an experience when they "saw the light," or made a great discovery about Jesus and themselves. They said, "Aha!" The person who invented the microchip said, "Aha!" when the discovery was made. You could show a chip in a digital watch if you wish. Then demonstrate that just as a lamp may be turned on when it is connected to the power, our light (or lives) can be turned on if we're connected to the power of God. Chat with the children about times when they've been turned on or when they've said, "Aha!" Enjoy their discoveries!

Prayer: Dear God, turn me on with your love. Amen.

The Season of Lent

No Trumpets!

Lesson 1: Joel 2:1–2, 12–17a
Lesson 2: 2 Corinthians 5:20b—6:2
Gospel: Matthew 6:1–6, 16–21

Theme: Genuine charity, prayer, and fasting
Resources: Trumpet; washable face paint; washcloth

Development: Ash Wednesday begins the season of Lent, when we recall Jesus' forty days of temptation in the wilderness alongside the Israelites' forty years of wilderness wandering. It is a time for reflection and for looking inside that anticipates its climax in the renewal of our covenant with God at Easter. The liturgical colors follow this pattern: Purple is used during Lent and changes dramatically to white on Easter.

All three readings open up the theme of covenant, a theme that runs through this period, with specific reference to our "religious" behavior. Joel the prophet sees the day of the Sovereign as a time of judgment and darkness and calls for a return to God who "is gracious and merciful, slow to anger, and abounding in steadfast love. . . . Blow the trumpet in Zion; sanctify a fast [Joel 2:13, 15]." Jesus, in the Gospel, describes genuine charity, prayer, and fasting and warns his hearers not to perform these acts for human approval.

Set the scene for the children by briefly introducing the season of Lent and stating Jesus' warning from the Gospel. Tell the story of these three segments, beginning with charity. Use a trumpet blast to vividly demonstrate the point. In the same way, pray with a loud voice, showing that praying like that is really "praying" to the crowd and not to God. To dramatize the teaching about fasting (you may have to give an explanation of fasting), put on some washable paint to

THE SEASON OF LENT 43

draw attention and then wash it off. Explain that God knows when we're genuinely giving to those in need or praying or fasting, and that God will reward us accordingly.

Prayer: Dear God, help me to do good things for you. Amen.

LENT 1

The Bow of Many Colors

Lesson 1: Genesis 9:8–17
Lesson 2: 1 Peter 3:18–22
Gospel: Mark 1:9–15

Theme: The covenant between God and humankind
Resource: Rainbow stickers—one for each person

Development: The story of Noah illustrates that God's covenant with Israel is the foundation of biblical religion. Children need to be exposed not only to the realities of people's faithlessness, reflected in the loss of life in the flood, but also to faithful persons of the Bible, so they will have some models with which to create their own personal covenant with God. The Old Testament lesson provides an excellent opportunity to introduce Noah, a man of great faith who obeyed God and received God's blessings. God says to Noah: "I set my bow in the cloud, and it shall be a sign of the covenant between me and the earth. . . . I will remember my covenant which is between me and you and every living creature of all flesh [Gen. 9:13, 15]." The rainbow is the sign of the covenant, a symbol and lifetime reminder of the covenant relationship between God and Noah and humankind.

Relate the story of God placing the rainbow in the

sky. Tell the children how good it is to know that the promises God has made will be kept. Point out that often we are unfaithful and give in to temptation, although Jesus set us an example of faithfulness when he was tempted and didn't sin. Baptism, like the rainbow, is also a sign of the covenant we make with God and is linked, in the second lesson, with the story of Noah. Affirm your love for the children and give each of them a rainbow sticker to remind them of your caring and of the covenant that God made long ago with Noah. A rainbow sticker on a bedroom window on a rainy day can be a powerful reminder!

Prayer: Wonderful Creator, thanks for rainbows. Amen.

LENT 2

Going for Gold

Lesson 1: Genesis 17:1–10, 15–19
Lesson 2: Romans 4:16–25
Gospel: Mark 8:31–38

Theme: The covenant with God demands total commitment.

Resource: "An Olympic Gold Medal"

Development: Abraham and Sarah are highlighted in the two lessons as examples of persons who are obedient to and blessed by God. They are described as the father (Genesis 17:4) and mother (Genesis 17:16) of nations, and their descendants inherit the everlasting covenant established between them and God. It is the complete faith of Abraham and Sarah that opens their lives to the possibilities of divine grace. The same total commitment is reflected in the Gospel when Jesus, speaking to the crowd, says: "If any would come after me, let them deny themselves and take up their own cross and follow me. For those who would save their life will lose it; and those who lose their life for my sake and the gospel's will save it [Mark 8:34–35]."

Approach this idea of commitment with the children by selecting a contemporary person who, by his or her attitude and action, demonstrates a total commitment. Then share that person's commitment. Better still, have that person come and share personally. For example, we have a good friend, David Guthrie, from Arkansas, who has a total commitment to winning an Olympic gold medal for the United States in the 200-meter breaststroke. He gets up early in the morning and trains several hours every day, building up his strength and stamina for world-class competition. He perfects his turns. He gives everything he's got to accomplish his dream. David is committed to going for gold!

Tie in your local example to Jesus' invitation to deny oneself, to be totally committed to Jesus, who gave his all for us.

Prayer: Dear God, I believe in you and I want to follow you. Amen.

Ten Rules to Remember

Lesson 1: Exodus 20:1–17
Lesson 2: 1 Corinthians 1:22–25
Gospel: John 2:13–22

Theme: Faithfulness to the covenant
Resource: Two "tablets"

Development: We continue the lenten theme of covenant by focusing on the aspect of faithfulness to the covenant, a major factor in any covenant relationship. During this season it is appropriate to recall our failure as individuals to live up to our promises to God.

In the Old Testament lesson we are reminded by God, the liberator, of the ten commandments, the basis of the covenant between God and the people. Commandments one to four are laws that deal with Israel's relationship to God. Commandments five to ten are laws that require fundamental responsibilities in human relationships. In short, the ten commandments are a summary of one's duty to God and to one's neighbor.

Using two "tablets" on which the commandments are printed, review the laws and indicate that God's ten rules to remember are to be obeyed. Children also need to be encouraged, at their level, to get rid of everything that stands in the way of fulfilling their covenant with God. There are indeed consequences for disobeying God, as illustrated by Jesus' angry response to the money-changers in the temple. Take care not to paint Jesus in a vindictive light. The motivation of Jesus' anger is love, and children need to be assured again and again that even when they do bad things, God still loves them.

Prayer: Dear God, thank you for loving me even when I do bad things. Amen.

LENT 4

The Biggest Hug Ever

Lesson 1: 2 Chronicles 36:14–23
Lesson 2: Ephesians 2:4–10
Gospel: John 3:14–21

Theme: God is love.
Resources: A globe and lots of hugs

Development: Today marks the midway point in the season of Lent. In some traditions this fourth Sunday is called "Refreshment Sunday." Yes, Lent can get "heavy," so here's a time to loosen up a little by using the theme of God is love as presented in John's Gospel and in Paul's letter to the Ephesians.

Zero in on John's statement: "For God so loved the world that God gave God's only Child, that whoever believes in that Child should not perish but have eternal life [John 3:16]." I have found this verse in the *Good News Bible* easier for children to understand: "For God loved the world so much that God gave God's only Child, so that everyone who believes in that Child may not die but have eternal life."

Impress on the children that God's love is for everyone in the world. By giving Jesus to us, God hugged the world with the biggest hug ever. Demonstrate this truth by hugging the globe, as if God were wrapping loving arms around all humankind. The children also need to know, experience, and literally hear that God's love in Christ is for them personally. God loves Suzanne and Robert and Meredith and. . . . As you say each child's name (name tags might be a good idea), hug her or him, if you feel comfortable with that. Suggest that after your prayer together the children might pass on God's love by hugging people in the congregation. Happy holy hugging!

Prayer: Dear God, thanks for loving me so much. I like hugs too! Amen.

LENT 5

All Wrapped Up

Lesson 1: Jeremiah 31:31–34
Lesson 2: Hebrews 5:7–10
Gospel: John 12:20–33

Theme: The new covenant in Christ
Resources: A caterpillar and cocoon

Development: The lessons today focus on the new covenant. Jeremiah foresees a new covenant that God will make with the people, a covenant written not on tablets of stone, but on human hearts. You may want to recall the "tablets" from the third Sunday of Lent to provide a smooth transition. The law that was "external" is now to be put within the people. Jesus also speaks of the new covenant in the Gospel, when he refers to his impending death and how his death is absolutely necessary in order to bring new life. He compares the process of divine salvation in this way: "Unless a grain of wheat falls into the earth and dies, it remains alone; but if it dies, it bears much fruit. They who love their life lose it, and they who hate their life in this world will keep it for eternal life [John 12:24–25]." Christians are called to die to all that prevents them from being faithful to their covenant. Death mysteriously brings new life. The reading from Hebrews confirms that the new covenant is made possible through the high priesthood of the risen Christ, a covenant made possible only through Christ's suffering and death.

Show the children a live caterpillar (or an enlarged picture of one), and share how it dies in its cocoon and later comes to life in the form of a butterfly. It gets all wrapped up and dies in order to live! Chat with the children about Jesus, who died for us in love and came to life again. On Easter this thought could be climaxed with the release of butterflies to represent the risen Christ.

Prayer: Loving God, thanks for caterpillars and cocoons and butterflies. Amen.

LENT 6—PALM SUNDAY

A Parade for Jesus

Lesson 1: Isaiah 50:4–9a
Lesson 2: Philippians 2:5–11
Gospel: Mark 11:1–11

Theme: Jesus' entry into Jerusalem
Resources: "Palm" branches—one for each child

Development: "Hosanna! . . . Hosanna in the highest! [Mark 11:9–10]." Even though these shouts of joy turned quickly into shouts of anger calling for Jesus' death, one can enable a sincere honoring of Jesus our Sovereign by recalling his entry into Jerusalem and his presence in our lives on Palm Sunday. A new realm and a new covenant were being established. It is indeed a day for a parade, an experience in which all of us, the people of God, can recognize Jesus as our leader and ourselves as his followers who share his love and mission.

Distribute palm branches to the children before the liturgy, and invite them to wave the branches and cheer as the choir processes during the opening hymn. A real colt carrying an appropriately dressed person can certainly add a vivid realism to the procession, if that is feasible in your situation.

During your conversation with the children point out that we were created to praise God and celebrate our love for God from day to day. Encourage them to take the palm branches (a sign of victory) home as a reminder of God's great love expressed in Jesus Christ and of the opportunity they have to celebrate that love each day. Ask them to share how they might celebrate God's love during the coming week.

Prayer: Dear God, it's fun to be in your parade! Amen.

MAUNDY THURSDAY

A Very Sad Supper

Lesson 1:   Exodus 24:3–8
Lesson 2:   1 Corinthians 10:16–17
Gospel: Mark 14:12–26

Theme: The Last Supper
Resources: Bread and "wine"

Development: Maundy Thursday, or Holy Thursday, is a day in Holy Week when we recall and dramatize the Last Supper. In many traditions the most obvious visual difference is that the altar and sanctuary are stripped of hangings and altar symbols. Although children may not be able to understand fully the implications of such a ritual, it is nonetheless important for them to hear what happened on that occasion when Jesus gathered with his friends for a meal.

Encourage them to imagine sharing the meal with the disciples, to be among them, and to feel through at their own level what was happening. Explain that it was Passover, the Jews' feast of thanksgiving for their deliverance from slavery in Egypt to the land of Canaan, and that it is celebrated to this day. Passover was supposed to be a joyous celebration, but it turned out to be a very sad supper. As Jesus and his disciples were eating, Jesus stated that one of the disciples would betray him and that it would be better if that man had not been born. The disciples were sad when they heard this, because they were his friends! How could his friends ever betray him? They were saddened even more when Jesus took bread and, after he had blessed and broken it, gave it to them, saying, "Take; this is my body [Mark 14:22]." Then Jesus took the cup. They all drank from it, and he said to them, "This is my blood of the covenant, which is poured out for many [Mark 14:24]."

A simple sharing of this supper, reenacted with bread and "wine," will enrich the children's appreciation of God's love in Jesus, whose body and blood were freely given. If your tradition permits them, as mine does, to actually participate in the reenactment, they will experience the gift of grace, the essence of the Last Supper.

Prayer: For bread and wine, your body and blood, we give you thanks, O God. Amen.

GOOD FRIDAY

Saying Good-bye

Lesson 1: Isaiah 52:13—53:12
Lesson 2: Hebrews 4:14–16; 5:7–9
Gospel: John 18:1—19:42

Theme: The crucifixion and death of Jesus

Resources: A cross; cocoons with butterflies rolled up inside for each child

Development: Good Friday provides an excellent opportunity to help children learn to say good-bye, a skill that is essential for personal growth. By hearing the story of Jesus' crucifixion and death told by faithful, caring people in the context of the Christian community, they will be enabled to see the tragic consequences of the sin of humankind in the light of God's grace. The Gospel lesson is a record of injustice, cruelty, hatred, and death. As such, it can be potentially frightening unless those relating to children demonstrate by their presence the hope of resurrection.

Gather with the children around the base of an upright cross. Indicate that on Good Friday we recall the great love of Jesus for us in dying for our sins and how difficult it was for Jesus' friends to say good-bye to him because they loved him so much. Proceed to share that sometimes it's difficult for us to say good-bye too, but that it's something we must learn to do. Explore some of the times from their experience when they've had to say good-bye, for example, when moving to another place or going off to school for the first time, or when a relative or pet has died. Assure them that God is always with us during those sometimes difficult and sad good-bye times.

Follow up the idea of dying in order to live by giving each child a sealed envelope containing a cocoon with a butterfly rolled up inside. Invite them to open the envelope on Easter morning. Let the "new life" surprise them!

Prayer: Dear God, I'm glad you're with me when I'm sad. Amen.

The Season of Easter

Easter Butterflies

Lesson 1: Isaiah 25:6–9
Lesson 2: 1 Corinthians 15:1–11
Gospel: Mark 16:1–8

Theme: The resurrection of Jesus
Resource: A "cloud" of suspended butterfly kites

Development: Easter Day marks the climax of the church year, and the season of Easter proclaims our hope in the resurrection of Jesus Christ. The three readings for today point to that hope and enlighten us to celebrate the mystery of God's grace and to live in the promise of eternal life. Isaiah, in the Old Testament lesson, describes the messianic banquet of all the nations of the world at which God promises to swallow up death forever and wipe away the tears from all the people's eyes. In the second lesson we have a record of the fulfillment of Isaiah's prophecy in the resurrection appearances of Jesus. And the Gospel recalls the experience of the women at the tomb when they learn the news of the resurrection.

This is a day for children particularly to experience the sheer joy of resurrection. Relate the exciting adventure of Mary Magdalene and Mary, the mother of Jesus, and Salome going to the tomb and their astonishment at the large stone being rolled away, their amazement that Jesus was not where he had been laid, and their fear as they came from the tomb. Then compare the caterpillar cocoon to the tomb. Suspend a "cloud" of butterfly kites or butterflies cut out of craft paper to intensify the image. Explain that just as the cocoon could not contain the butterfly, so the tomb could not contain Jesus. Easter butterflies are symbols of Jesus' resurrection.

Prayer: Dear God, on Easter Day, we thank you for butterflies and for Jesus, who is alive again! Amen.

EASTER 2

Shalom

Lesson 1: Acts 4:32–35
Lesson 2: 1 John 1:1—2:2
Gospel: John 20:19–31

Theme: Peace
Resource: The word shalom printed on newsprint

Development: The readings for this Easter season follow a pattern. The first lesson from Acts shows the continued work of the resurrected Christ in the church, and the second lesson, readings from 1 John, emphasize the direct connection between loving God and loving our neighbor. The Gospel readings record resurrection appearances and expand our image of Jesus and the church.

Today I would suggest, among the many possibilities, using the theme of peace or shalom. In an age when peace seems so elusive it is good to remind ourselves of God's gift of peace to the world. The Gospel cites two resurrection appearances of Jesus to the disciples, and in each case Jesus greets them with the phrase "Peace be with you [John 20:19, 26]."

Print the word shalom on a piece of newsprint or bristol board, and explore the meaning and implications of this word with the children. Shalom means wholeness, well-being, justice, health, and love. It is a common greeting when meeting or leaving a person. It is the condition to be fostered among all people. We, as believers in the risen Christ, are committed to seeking peace for ourselves and, as the lesson from 1 John indicates, for our neighbors.

Form a circle, join hands, and have a circle dance using the song "Shalom." The text of the song is as follows: "Shalom my friends, Shalom my friends, Shalom. Shalom. We'll see you again. We'll see you again. Shalom. Shalom."* Encourage the children to greet one another with "Shalom" in the coming week.

Prayer: Dear God, thank you for your gift of peace. Shalom. Amen.

*English by Augustus D. Zanzig. Copyright © 1957 by World Around Songs, Inc. Used with permission.

EASTER 3

The Family Book

Lesson 1: Acts 3:12–19
Lesson 2: 1 John 3:1–7
Gospel: Luke 24:35–48

Theme: God opens our minds to understand the scriptures.

Resources: Family Bible; bookmarks for each child

Development: The Gospel recalls how Jesus showed himself to his disciples and "opened their minds to understand the scriptures [Luke 24:45]" that revealed his death and resurrection. "Thus it is written, that the Christ should suffer and on the third day rise from the dead, and that repentance and forgiveness of sins should be preached in his name to all nations [Luke 24:46–47]."

To get at the theme of God opening our minds to understand the scriptures, try a riddle. What's usually big and heavy, inspired by God, contains lots of chapters, and belongs to a family? Show a big family

Bible, and indicate how families consider this book a special gift from God. The importance of the scriptures to Jesus and his disciples and the church and us must be impressed on the minds and hearts of the children. Although we do not want to promote worshiping of the scriptures, we do want to encourage a healthy appreciation of the inspired word of God. In liturgy and at home the scriptures are a key tool in our fulfilling God's love as children of God, as described in the second lesson, and in fulfilling the mandate to preach the gospel as Peter does to the people of Jerusalem, as related in the first lesson.

The spirit of the resurrected Christ helps us to understand the scriptures and cultivate an attitude of openness essential to hear the words of eternal life as the Bible is read daily. Just as Jesus opened the disciples' minds to understand the scriptures, so God opens our minds when we read the Bible.

Turn to the Gospel reading in the family Bible, and read the passage with the children. To reinforce the theme, a Bible bookmark could be given to each child to use in his or her own Bible at home.

Prayer: Dear God, thank you for the Bible. Amen.

EASTER 4

The Good Shepherd

Lesson 1: Acts 4:8–12
Lesson 2: 1 John 3:18–24
Gospel: John 10:11–18

Theme: The image of Jesus as the good shepherd
Resources: A sheep; shepherd's clothing; a staff

Development: Jesus said, "I am the good shepherd [John 10:11]." In Jesus' day, in a pastoral setting, the image of a shepherd would have been easily understood. But today, when our cities of concrete and steel seem so removed from sheep and shepherds, we need time to absorb the full impact and meaning of the image. Jesus, the good shepherd, is still a powerful description!

Surprise the children today by having a live sheep, by dressing as a shepherd, and by carrying a shepherd's staff, or crook, the symbol of caring. If you have a "real" shepherd in your congregation or area, perhaps that person would be willing to lead the conversation. The very presence of a live sheep will certainly open up the theme.

Tell Jesus' story in your own words, noting primarily that the good shepherd knows the sheep and they know him. Assure the children of God's personal care for them and that just as the shepherd knows each sheep by name, so God knows their names and cares for them individually. In this Easter season remind them that God loved them so much that Jesus died for them, just like the shepherd who risks his or her life to save one of the sheep. Also point out that the sheep know the shepherd. The children need to learn about Jesus, the good shepherd, so that they can take care of other people.

Prayer: Dear God, thank you for sheep and Jesus, the good shepherd. Amen.

EASTER 5

Special Branches

Lesson 1: Acts 8:26–40
Lesson 2: 1 John 4:7–12
Gospel: John 15:1–8

Theme: The image of Jesus as the true vine

Resource: Vine (or plant)

Development: Last week we considered Jesus as the good shepherd. Today we want to move on to see Jesus in a different light.

Show the children a vine (or plant), and point out that Jesus said, "I am the vine, you are the branches [John 15:5]." Inquire what they think that might mean. Jesus describes himself as the vine to which each branch must be united if it is to bear fruit. He describes the Creator as the vinedresser who not only creates, but also sustains the life of the vine.

Explain that while pruning the vine the vinedresser prunes the branches that produce fruit so that they can produce more. The key is that the branches have to be connected to the vine so that the life-giving energy in the vine can flow through to the branches. If the branches are not connected, they will not receive the necessary energy, will not produce fruit, and will die. Jesus is the vine and we are the special branches. Express that God's love is strong, and that we can keep growing faithfully if we remain connected to the true vine! Note: You may want to invite a person who is familiar with vines to assist you in this conversation.

Prayer: Dear Jesus, I'm growing with you! Amen.

EASTER 6

Magic Penny

Lesson 1: Acts 10:44–48
Lesson 2: 1 John 5:1–6
Gospel: John 15: 9–17

Theme: Love one another.

Resources: New pennies

Development: Love is the theme in the second lesson and Gospel on this sixth Sunday of Easter. In 1 John it is pointed out that in baptism believers become children of God, with the responsibility to love God and their neighbors. The Gospel records Jesus' commandment: "Love one another as I have loved you [John 15:12]."

Share with the children how God has set an example of loving for us to follow in Jesus Christ, who offered his life for us all. "Greater love has no one than this," said Jesus, "that one lay down one's life for one's friends [John 15:13]." The great affirmation is that God is love! Jesus invites his hearers and us to keep the commandments, just as he did, so that we can abide or remain in his love and be joyful. The commandments are seen here not as restrictive, but as liberating.

Indicate that God has called us as friends and has chosen us to care for and love others. Give each child a shiny "magic" penny, symbolic of love. To emphasize this final idea, sing "Magic Penny": "Love is something if you give it away, give it away, give it away. O, love is something if you give it away, You'll end up having more. It's just like a magic penny, hold it tight and you won't have any. Lend it, spend it and you'll have so many, they'll roll all over the floor. O, love is something if you give it away, give it away, give it away. O, love is something if you give it away, You'll end up having more!"*

Prayer: Dear God, thank you for your love. I love you too. Amen.

*"Magic Penny," by Malvina Reynolds. © Copyright 1955, 1958 by Northern Music Company, New York, NY. Used by permission. All rights reserved.

Mission Possible!

Lesson 1: Acts 1:15–17, 21–26
Lesson 2: 1 John 5:9–13
Gospel: John 17:11b–19

Theme: The unity of the church and its mission
Resources: Two or three beach balls (or balloons)

Development: Today's readings focus on discipleship and the prayer of Jesus for the church. The lesson from Acts describes how Matthias is chosen to fill the vacancy left by Judas. The epistle of 1 John encourages the disciples to believe with confidence that their prayers are heard and that they have eternal life. Discipleship is to be lived out in the world from the context of the church, which Jesus describes in the Gospel.

Enable the children to gain an appreciation for the church as people. Point out that the earnest desire of Jesus is that the people "be one, even as we [God and Jesus] are one [John 17:11]." The church as the body of Christ is to work together, or cooperate, to accomplish its mission to proclaim the Easter message of good news of God's love.

Illustrate the cooperative nature of the church by taking a beach ball or balloon and inviting two persons to hold it without using their arms. Extend the illustration by using three balls and three persons or other combinations. If you are not relating to the children in a liturgical setting, you may want to try any cooperative game involving the whole group. Emphasize that when the people cooperated they were able to hold onto the balls, just as we will be able to accomplish our mission when we cooperate with one another as the body of Christ, the church. Mission Possible!

Prayer: Dear God, we will be one with you to make your mission possible. Amen.

The Season of
Pentecost

The Church's Birthday

Lesson 1: Acts 2:1–21
Lesson 2: Romans 8:22–27
Gospel: John 15:26–27; 16:4b–15

Theme: The coming of the Holy Spirit
Resources: Red, helium-filled balloons with strings

Development: Pentecost is a celebration of our covenant relationship with God, a relationship made known originally through the ancient covenant of the Old Testament and now through the abiding power and presence of the Holy Spirit in our lives. The work of the risen Christ is seen in the gift of the Spirit that replaces the law as the basis of life in the community.

Truly celebrate this day with the children by sharing the story in Acts 2. It's a marvelous story and, when read with faithful understanding and feeling, will speak for itself. Focus on two things: First, note that Pentecost (literally, fifty days) marks the reception of the Holy Spirit, an exciting event symbolized by the liturgical color red. Second, note that Pentecost marks the beginning of the dynamic missionary life of the Christian church.

Celebrate the birthday of the church! Near the close of your conversation with the children, have someone dressed in red deliver a "singing teleballoonogram." Sing happy birthday to the church, and give each child a red balloon with the encouragement to go, like the early church in its mission, and share the excitement of Pentecost with friends and neighbors.

Prayer: Dear God, Pentecost and red balloons are fun! Amen.

What Does God Do?

Lesson 1: Isaiah 6:1–8
Lesson 2: Romans 8:12–17
Gospel: John 3:1–17

Theme: The Trinity
Resource: A triangle

Development: Trinity Sunday offers an excellent opportunity to acquaint children with the wholeness of God by describing what God does and the ways in which we experience God's presence. All three readings point to God, who meets people in their everyday lives. Isaiah has a vision and responds to God's invitation by committing himself to go. Paul urges the church at Rome to be moved by God's Spirit and not be enslaved to death so that they may become children and heirs with Christ. Moreover, John records in his Gospel how Jesus and Nicodemus have a conversation about the "second" birth.

Use a large triangle, representing the Trinity, to describe the three major activities of God. God creates, loves, and inspires. God created the universe and us and continues to create in us today. God showed love in the person of Jesus Christ, who gave the ultimate sign of love by dying on the cross. God continues to share love by supporting and caring for us each day. And God inspires us by the Holy Spirit to discover who God is and who we are together in the world. Elaborate on these three activities and how we experience them by asking questions if you like. Enable the children to see that, although we will never fully understand God, the Trinity is one way we can describe what we do know about God.

Prayer: Dear God, thank you for creating, loving, and inspiring me. Amen.

How's Your Heart?

Lesson 1:   1 Samuel 16:1–13
Lesson 2:   2 Corinthians 4:5–12
Gospel: Mark 2:23—3:6

Theme: The anointing of David as king
Resource: An anatomical heart

Development: From now on in the season of Pentecost, I usually will choose only one of the lessons on which to base a conversation, because the *Common Lectionary* has not selected readings that have a thematic unity for each day.

From the Old Testament lesson today records the anointing of David as king. Tell the story in abbreviated form, and then focus on the statement of Yahweh to Samuel: "Do not look on his appearance or on the height of his stature, because I have rejected him; for the Sovereign sees not as humankind sees; humankind looks on the outward appearance, but the Sovereign looks on the heart [1 Sam. 16:7]." Explain that God is not so much concerned about appearances, what a person looks like, as with what's inside a person, how a person really feels or what is in her or his heart.

Show the children an anatomical heart. Indicate how essential the heart is to the body's functioning well and that, in fact, a person's heart determines whether or not he or she lives. Point out that when we give our hearts to God, our hearts are really in the right place and we're living the life God gives us from the inside out.

Prayer: Dear God, I love you with my whole heart. Amen.

Forever and Ever

Lesson 1: 1 Samuel 16:14–23
Lesson 2: 2 Corinthians 4:13—5:1
Gospel: Mark 3:20–35

Theme: The Christian trusts in things that are unseen.
Resource: An antique chair

Development: Paul, in the second lesson, speaks to the church at Corinth about the eternal and glorious hope that belongs to Jesus' disciples even in trouble and death. To those who believe, he asserts, the resurrection of Christ is a constant source of comfort and sustaining power, especially for those who suffer illness. We have hope, says Paul, "because we look not to the things that are seen but to the things that are unseen; for the things that are seen are transient, but the things that are unseen are eternal [2 Cor. 4:18]."

Enable the children to appreciate, at their level, this fundamental mystery of Christian faith by using an antique chair. Explain that the chair is useful and valuable and has lasted for a long time, but that it is unlikely the chair will last thousands of years. Point out that, as Christians, we are not to put our trust in things that are seen, because such things last for only a while. Rather, we should put our trust in invisible things, like love, kindness, patience, compassion, joy, that last forever and ever. Our hope is in the God who was in the beginning, is now, and who will be forever!

Prayer: Dear God, even though I can't see you, I trust you. Amen.

Small Is OK with God

Lesson 1: 2 Samuel 1:1, 17–27
Lesson 2: 2 Corinthians 5:6–10, 14–17
Gospel: Mark 4:26–34

Theme: The parable of the mustard seed
Resources: Seed and resulting bush or tree; mustard seed necklaces for each child

Development: What is the realm of God like? "It is like a grain of mustard seed," said Jesus, "which, when sown upon the ground, is the smallest of all the seeds on earth; yet when it is sown it grows up and becomes the greatest of all shrubs, and puts forth large branches, so that the birds of the air can make nests in its shade [Mark 4:31–32]." The children can relate to and identify with this great parable immediately, because the mustard seed is small like them.

Tell the parable, using a small seed and the resulting bush or tree, if possible. Try to use a seed that is known in your area. Our church happens to be located in the middle of an apple orchard, so an apple seed was the obvious choice. Explain that in God's realm, we are enabled to grow from small beginnings. Small is OK with God. We must take care of ourselves, however, just as we take care of the growing seed by watering, cultivating, and fertilizing it. God, who is the creator of all things and us, loves us at every stage of our growth. Children need to be assured that God loves them right now, when they're little, and not just when they grow up to be adults. A good way to reinforce this parable's message is to give each child a necklace strung with a mustard seed in a plastic container. This will serve as a good affirming reminder.

Prayer: Wonderful Creator, thanks for seeds that grow. I'm growing too—for you! Amen.

PENTECOST 5

Swing Now!

Lesson 1: 2 Samuel 5:1–12
Lesson 2: 2 Corinthians 5:18—6:2
Gospel: Mark 4:35–41

Theme: Being at one with God
Resources: A baseball and bat

Development: The focus of the second lesson today is reconciliation. Paul celebrates God's reconciling work through Christ's love and sacrificial death and indicates that, as Christians, we are the agents of reconciliation. He concludes: "Behold, now is the acceptable time; behold, now is the day of salvation [2 Cor. 6:2]."

Share with the children that they can be at one with God now. They don't have to wait until they grow up. God's gift of life is to be enjoyed now. Illustrate this "nowness" of salvation by using a baseball and bat. Show how the batter, in order to hit the ball, must swing the bat right when the ball comes. If the batter swings too early or too late, he or she won't hit the ball. The batter has to swing now! Remind them that God loved them so much that Jesus died and rose so that they could give their hearts to God today.

Prayer: Dear God, thanks for loving me today. I love you right now too. Amen.

PENTECOST 6

The Haves and the Have-Nots

Lesson 1: 2 Samuel 6:1–15
Lesson 2: 2 Corinthians 8:7–15
Gospel: Mark 5:21–43

Theme: Sharing with the poor
Resources: Six bread rolls

Development: The second lesson provides an excellent base on which to build a conversation about sharing with the poor. Paul records that Christ has set us the true example of generosity: "Though he was rich, yet for your sake he became poor, so that by his poverty you might become rich [2 Cor. 8:9]." Impress on the children the graciousness of Christ in offering himself for us all so we could live. Note that Paul uses Christ's example as he urges the church at Corinth to take up a collection, as much as they could afford, for the poor Christians in Jerusalem.

Illustrate Christ's example of sharing by dividing the children into two groups: the Haves (a few children) and the Have-Nots (many children). While giving five rolls to the Haves and one roll to the Have-Nots, indicate that this is how food is distributed in the world. Explore with them how it feels to be in each group and how they might work out the problem of the Haves having more than enough to eat and the Have-Nots not having enough. You may want to conclude today's conversation by indicating how your congregation shares with the poor.

Prayer: Dear God, thanks for all you give me. I want to share like Jesus. Amen.

b's and d's

Lesson 1: 2 Samuel 7:1–17
Lesson 2: 2 Corinthians 12:1–10
Gospel: Mark 6:1–6

Theme: God's power is made perfect in weakness.
Resource: The letters b and d on poster board

Development: The epistle lesson reveals Paul's discovery of strength that comes through weakness. God says to Paul: "My grace is sufficient for you, for my power is made perfect in weakness [2 Cor. 12:9]." That's good news for all of us, especially children, who need to hear that it's all right to fail, all right to make a mistake, all right not to be perfect. They need to know that God wants them to have the courage to try, and that they will not be punished if they make an error. Point out that it is by making mistakes that they find out what they need to work on or improve.

Develop the theme by noting that children, when they're learning to print, often confuse b and d. Use large b and d letters to show how similar they are and how easy it is for them to be mixed up. Remind the children that almost everyone straightens out this difficulty quickly by trying to put the b where the b is supposed to be and the d where the d is supposed to be. Assure them that God loves them even when they make mistakes.

Prayer: Dear God, help me to keep trying, even when I make mistakes. Amen.

Not Welcome

Lesson 1: 2 Samuel 7:18–29
Lesson 2: Ephesians 1:1–10
Gospel: Mark 6:7–13

Theme: Disciples of Jesus are sometimes rejected.
Resource: A NOT WELCOME sign

Development: In the Gospel today Jesus calls the disciples and sends them out two by two with authority over the unclean spirits. He calls them to a life of power but also to a life of struggle and confrontation with the world. With this in mind he gives them some helpful instructions. He encourages them to take on their mission only the really important things. Don't get burdened with a lot of nonessentials. He warns them not to let their desire for comfort draw their attention away from their task. Jesus also says: "And if any place will not receive you and they refuse to hear you, when you leave, shake off the dust that is on your feet for a testimony against them [Mark 6:11]."

Focus on the last "instruction" with the children by using a NOT WELCOME sign. Explain that the disciples sometimes went to a town or a house in which they weren't welcome, and that sometimes in our lives we meet people who won't receive us. Every time I see a BEWARE OF DOG sign on a gatepost I have a similar feeling of being unwelcome.

Express that it's natural to feel disappointment when we are rejected, and that we are not responsible for the actions of others. We are not responsible for results, that is, that people will like us, but for our efforts. When we do meet rejection or defeat while doing God's will, we need to move on in the spirit of trust that Jesus demonstrated in his life.

Prayer: Dear God, help me to show your love even if it means somebody won't like me. Amen.

PENTECOST 9

Sandals

Lesson 1: 2 Samuel 11:1–15
Lesson 2: Ephesians 2:11–22
Gospel: Mark 6:30–34

Theme: Compassion
Resources: Two pairs of sandals

Development: Mark's Gospel records how the apostles came back to Jesus to report on their progress regarding their teaching and other activities. Jesus, noticing that they were exhausted and realizing that they hardly had had time to eat, went away with them in a boat to an isolated place to be by themselves and rest.

Everyone will be able to identify with the idea of vacation here because the ninth Sunday of Pentecost is in midsummer. Begin today by linking the idea of their vacation with the initial part of the Gospel. Move on to explain that the crowd went ahead on land, and when Jesus and the apostles arrived at their destination, the crowd was already waiting for them. The key point to make is that Jesus, when he saw all the people, even though he too was tired, "had compassion on them, because they were like sheep without a shepherd; and he began to teach them many things [Mark 6:34]." The Good Shepherd took pity on and taught them because he felt what it was like to be them, or to put himself in their "sandals."

Demonstrate this last image by using one small pair and one large pair of sandals that belong to people in the congregation, and explore with the children what it might be like to walk in these shoes.

Prayer: Dear God, thanks for vacations. Help me to care, like Jesus, for all people. Amen.

PENTECOST 10

Rooted in Love

Lesson 1: 2 Samuel 12:1–14
Lesson 2: Ephesians 3:14–21
Gospel: John 6:1–15

Theme: The love of Christ
Resource: A tree with a substantial root ball

Development: The readings for today offer several possibilities. I have chosen to focus on the theme of the love of Christ in Paul's letter to the Ephesians. Paul begins the passage by indicating that every family in heaven and on earth has a common ancestry in God, our parent, and that it is the riches of God's glory that strengthen the inner person to discern the truth. He expresses the deep desire that Christ may live in the hearts of the Christians in Ephesus through their faith. He also expresses the desire "that you, being rooted and grounded in love, may have power to comprehend with all the saints what is the breadth and length and height and depth, and to know the love of Christ which surpasses knowledge, that you may be filled with all the fulness of God [Eph. 3:17–19]."

Enable the children to understand what it means to be "rooted and grounded in love" and therefore "filled with all the fulness of God." Demonstrate how the roots of a tree have to go down deep and spread out to provide a strong, solid foundation for the tree. Expose and examine the root ball. Explain that when the roots are placed firmly in the ground, the tree can withstand the wind and weather and can grow to its full potential. Draw the analogy that people, like trees, have to be rooted firmly in the love of Christ so that they can grow to their full potential.

Paul concludes with a frequently used benediction (below) that could be used as a closing prayer.

Prayer: "Now to God who by the power at work within us is able to do far more abundantly than all that we ask or think, to God be glory in the church and in Christ Jesus to all generations, for ever and ever. Amen [Eph. 3:20–21]."

The Bread of Life

Lesson 1: 2 Samuel 12:15b–24
Lesson 2: Ephesians 4:1–6
Gospel: John 6:24–35

Theme: Jesus, the bread of life
Resource: A loaf of bread

Development: Earlier in the year we considered two "I am" statements of Jesus: "I am the good shepherd [John 10:11]" on Easter 4, and "I am the true vine [John 15:1]" on Easter 5. Today we examine a third: "I am the bread of life [John 6:35]." Jesus refers to himself in this way in response to the crowd who followed him after the feeding of the five thousand, looking for more bread to eat. Christ tells them not to work for bread that spoils, but for food that lasts for eternal life. Jesus said: "I am the bread of life; whoever comes to me shall not hunger, and whoever believes in me shall never thirst [John 6:35]."

This Sunday focus on the bread as the symbol for Jesus. Explain that bread is essential in everyone's diet and that it satisfies physical hunger. Ask the children if they have ever been really hungry. Jesus knew how important bread was so he compared himself to it. Jesus, the bread of life, is really food for the soul. If we believe in and feed ourselves with Jesus, the eternal bread, God promises that we will never again go hungry! Point out that in the eucharist we take bread, the symbol of Jesus' body broken for us, and recall God's promise and believe!

Prayer: Dear God, thank you for the bread we eat; thank you for Jesus, the Bread of life! Amen.

PENTECOST 12

The Imitators

Lesson 1: 2 Samuel 18:1, 5, 9–15
Lesson 2: Ephesians 4:25—5:2
Gospel: John 6:35, 41–51

Theme: Christian attitude and behavior
Resource: A full-length mirror

Development: Paul urges the Christians at Ephesus, in the epistle lesson today, to reflect what Christ did for them through their own attitudes and relationships. They are to be angry but not sin, perform honest work, speak graciously, and "be kind to one another, tenderhearted, forgiving one another, as God in Christ forgave [them] [Eph. 4:32]." The quality of love that is demonstrated in Jesus, Paul insists, is to be the ruling principle in their lives. Open the minds and hearts of the children to these thoughts by referring to Paul's conclusion of the passage: "Therefore be imitators of God, as beloved children. And walk in love, as Christ loved us and gave himself up for us [Eph. 5:1–2]."

Note how children often imitate their parents or a teacher or a famous person. Indicate that the model Paul was recommending to the Ephesians was Christ, who set us the example of love by giving himself for us on the cross.

The image here goes far beyond "copying." Using a full-length mirror, point out that when we look in the mirror we see a reflection of ourselves. God wants us to be what we were created to be—ourselves—and to show in our attitudes and behavior (suggestions above in Ephesians 4:32) that we belong to Christ. When people look at us they will be able to see us and the loving Christ within us. Encourage the children to internalize the love of Christ so they can reflect that great love in their lives.

Prayer: Dear God, help me to reflect your great love in Jesus. Amen.

PENTECOST 13

One Day to Live

Lesson 1: 2 Samuel 18:24–33
Lesson 2: Ephesians 5:15–20
Gospel: John 6:51–58

Theme: Time
Resource: A day from your diary

Development: Begin your conversation today by asking the children what they would do if they had only one day to live. You might want to share what you would do too. Listen closely to their answers, noting that what they have answered is probably most important to them. Relate how the new Christians in Ephesus were encouraged to use their time: "Look carefully then how you walk, not as unwise people but as wise, making the most of the time [Eph. 5:15]." Paul said that the key to making the most of their time was to be filled with the Spirit.

Point out that God gives each of us the same amount of time and entrusts us with the responsibility of choosing how to use it. Then "honestly" share a day from your diary, using your personal calendar. Explain how you chose to use your time on that day. If you wish and if it's true for you, confess that occasionally you know you could have used your time more wisely. Include in your sharing things like playing, working, sleeping, family activities, doing nothing, eating, and doing a job around the house. Help the children to see that they have a choice right now in their lives as to how they will use the time God has given them. Chat with them about how they may use their time wisely tomorrow.

Prayer: Dear God, I want to use my time wisely for you. Amen.

PENTECOST 14

Bread and Beads

Lesson 1: 2 Samuel 23:1–7
Lesson 2: Ephesians 5:21–33
Gospel: John 6:55–69

Theme: Care for one another as God cares for you.
Resources: A wedding ring or band; a pair of sneakers with "friendship beads"

Development: The second lesson and the Gospel combine today to enlighten our understanding of covenant relationships. In the Gospel, Jesus calls people into covenant with him, and to those who believe in him he promises eternal life. Paul, in the epistle lesson, says that the relationship between Christ and the church is a model for husband and wife relations.

Because children will have considerable difficulty gleaning a direct understanding of these passages, I suggest dealing with the related theme of friendship. Chat with them about the importance of friendship and what qualities they think a good friend should have. Explore how Jesus set us an example of caring for one another in a special way, with particular reference to Jesus giving his life for us as the supreme sign of friendship.

Indicate that we use the bread in the eucharist as a symbol of Jesus' caring and of our "eternal" friendship. Show how we symbolize our friendship covenants today by using a wedding ring and a pair of sneakers with friendship beads pinned to the laces. You may want to give away some beads. If you get some in return, remember that the children will expect you to wear the beads they gave you.

Prayer: Dear God, thank you for Jesus who showed us how to be friends. Amen.

It's What's Inside That Really Matters

Lesson 1: 1 Kings 2:1–4, 10–12
Lesson 2: Ephesians 6:10–20
Gospel: Mark 7:1–8, 14–15, 21–23

Theme: The inner person
Resources: Two balloons; string; helium

Development: The Gospel and the second lesson present the theme of the inner person. Jesus, in the Gospel, encounters the religious leaders—the scribes and the Pharisees—and denounces them as hypocrites for ignoring the genuine commandment of God and keeping the traditions created by people. He quotes to them Isaiah's prophecy: "This people honors me with their lips, but their heart is far from me; in vain do they worship me, teaching as doctrine the precepts of humankind [Mark 7:6–7]." Paul continues the theme by urging the Christians in Ephesus to "put on the whole armor of God [Eph. 6:11]," so that they may stand firmly when they contend with the forces of evil. The armor, which is external in nature, is really an internal strengthening that includes truth, righteousness, peace, faith, salvation, the Spirit, and prayer. The overall result is God's ambassador who proclaims boldly from within the mystery of the gospel.

Chat briefly with the children about the two lessons, focusing on the importance of what's inside a person, what a person believes, and how that determines a person's actions. Demonstrate this truth graphically by blowing up two balloons—one with air and the other with helium—and tying a string to each one. Ask the children to explain why one balloon falls to the ground and the other floats. You will have enabled them to discover the Christian principle that it's what's inside that really matters!

Prayer: Dear God, fill me up with your love so I can live for you. Amen.

Do It! Do It! Do It!

Lesson 1: Proverbs 2:1–8
Lesson 2: James 1:17–27
Gospel: Mark 7:31–37

Theme: Hearing and doing the word
Resources: Newsprint and marker; a stop sign

Development: The letter of James is a series of practical instructions on how to live the Christian life. In the passage we are reading today the writer addresses the matter of Christian worship and its resulting action.

Ask the children why they came to worship God today. Record their answers on newsprint to indicate that you are listening carefully and taking their answers seriously. Note with them that one of the chief reasons we worship is to receive or to listen to God's word, and that James suggested how we are to listen: eagerly, with open ears, patiently (think before you speak), and not jump to conclusions.

Then share James's invitation to be "doers of the word, and not hearers only [James 1:22]." Explain that, as Christians, not only do we need to listen when we worship, but also to apply what we hear in our lives at home and school and play when we leave worship. Illustrate this idea by using a stop sign. If a person hears that people must obey this sign by stopping, then that person should actually stop when he or she sees the sign. Go on to give other illustrations. If we hear in worship that we must take care of the poor, or repent of our sin, or love our neighbor, or visit the sick, then we've got to show by our actions that we are doers of the word and not hearers only. Select practical, specific examples in your local setting that will bring this thought to life.

Prayer: Dear God, I listened to your word today and want to do it this week. Amen.

PENTECOST 17

Follow the Leader

Lesson 1: Proverbs 22:1–2, 8–9
Lesson 2: James 2:1–5, 8–10, 14–17
Gospel: Mark 8:27–38

Theme: Following Jesus
Resources: Two backpacks—one adult- and one child-size; "printed cards"

Development: The Gospel offers a variety of possibilities for today, and one must be sensitive not to inflict information or motivation overload. Introduce the idea of following Jesus and its implications by pointing out that Jesus, at this critical point in his ministry, asked his disciples who others as well as they themselves thought he was and how they responded. Share the dramatic movement from the question of Jesus' identity asked of "others" and of the question addressed to the individual disciples. Note Peter's declaration of faith.

Then focus on Jesus' statement about following

him: "If any would come after me, let them deny themselves and take up their own cross and follow me [Mark 8:34]." Tie in this statement with Follow the Leader, a game with which all children are familiar. Recall that in order to play this game you have to know and trust the leader and do what the leader wants you to do. Indicate that the Christian life could be compared to this game, in which Jesus is the leader and we are the followers who are expected to do what Jesus wants: deny ourselves and take up our cross, like him. Demonstrate Jesus' expectations of denial and cross-bearing by putting on an adult-size backpack and inviting a child to put on a child-size backpack. Explain that the backpack is like a cross, and that God gives us all the strength we need to carry it and never expects us to carry more than we can handle.

Before the conversation, to enable an understanding of cross-bearing in the lives of children, print examples of cross-bearing—loving, caring, sharing, accepting, forgiving—on cards and put them in the child-size backpack. Take the cards out now and show them to the children. Conclude today with a simple invitation to follow Jesus.

Prayer: Dear Jesus, I want to follow you and carry my cross like you. Amen.

PENTECOST 18

Running Together

Lesson 1:   Job 28:20–28
Lesson 2:   James 3:13–18
Gospel: Mark 9:30–37

Theme: Life in God's realm
Resource: Ribbons

Development: Today's Gospel is the central core of Jesus' teaching on the meaning of life and the nature of the realm of God: "If any one would be first, that person must be last of all and servant of all [Mark 9:35]." Jesus urged his disciples to engage in a servant ministry. Convey this fundamental teaching of Jesus about servanthood by telling the story as recorded in the Gospel, noting how Jesus tells of his death and resurrection, the supreme evidence of servanthood, and how the disciples discussed among themselves who was the greatest. Point out that the disciples were really concerned about their status in the new realm and that Jesus responded to their concern for power, honor, and prestige by stating that the greatest people in his realm were the ones who were humble and willing to serve.

Explore the theme further by using the image of a running race at a church picnic or at school. Indicate that in such races the ribbon is awarded to the person who crosses the finish line first. The focus here is clearly on winning by being first and appropriately so because that's the rule of that race. But in God's "human race" it's radically different! It's a cooperative race in which the "winner" is the one who is humble and willing to serve. Instead of the runners competing to be first, they help and support one another and run hand in hand by God's love. In God's race, it doesn't matter if one is a child or an adult, a president or a janitor, a student or a teacher. The most important thing to God is that we be humble like servants and innocent like children. Reinforce the latter idea and affirm each child's specialness by giving her or him a ribbon as a reminder of God's "human race" and her or his place in it.

Prayer: Dear God, help me to run for you in love. Amen.

Instant Breakfast

Lesson 1: Job 42:1–6
Lesson 2: James 4:13–17; 5:7–11
Gospel: Mark 9:38–50

Theme: Patience
Resources: Instant breakfast; seeds and the resulting crop

Development: The theme of the second lesson is patience, another characteristic of Christian behavior cited by James. The patience he specifically refers to is in relation to the coming of the Sovereign.

In this age of almost instant everything, children need to hear the message of James and incorporate it into their lives. Psychologists have described the present generation as knowing what it wants and wanting those things now!

Today, mix an instant breakfast and then, with the children's assistance, make a list of "instants" in their lives: instant-on TV, instant replay, instant hot chocolate, and so on. In contrast to these "instants" suggest that sometimes in our lives we have to be patient, that we can't have everything right away, that sometimes we just have to wait, like the farmer, who has to be patient because it's a long time between seedtime (show some seeds) and harvest (show the final crop if it's available). Note that the farmer is still busy cultivating, weeding, fertilizing, and watering while the crop is growing. Sometimes impatience is born of inactivity.

If you think it is necessary, use another analogy to reinforce your point. For example, some children who receive an allowance save diligently, waiting patiently and postponing gratification until the day when they can purchase their "heart's desire." Encourage the children to be patient in the coming week.

Prayer: O God, we confess that sometimes we are impatient. Help us to be patient this week. Amen.

PENTECOST 20

All People Are Special

Lesson 1: Genesis 2:18–24
Lesson 2: Hebrews 1:1–4; 2:9–11
Gospel: Mark 10:2–16

Theme: The realm of God belongs to all God's people.
Resources: An adult for every child

Development: Today provides a splendid opportunity to celebrate, children and adults together! This may be difficult to do in some Christian communities because the reality is that children are not always accorded the same personal rights as adults, nor are they fully appreciated as God's children. Indeed, with courage, you may be able to begin a new day for the child and the adult in your church!

Invite the children to ask adults to come with them for their conversation. Relate the story from the Gospel, beginning at verse 13. Explain to them the blindness of the disciples to the worth of a child and the qualities Jesus recognized in children: dependence, receptivity, and spontaneity, that is, the capacity to act immediately according to what they understand.

Note that Jesus confirmed the specialness of children by declaring that the realm of God belonged to them and to those who received them. As a sign that the realm of God belongs to all God's people— children and adults—form a circle, join hands, and pray together.

Prayer: Dear God, we thank you for children and adults. We thank you that the realm of God is ours! Amen.

A Tight Squeeze

Lesson 1: Genesis 3:8–19
Lesson 2: Hebrews 4:1–3, 9–13
Gospel: Mark 10:17–30

Theme: Discipleship
Resources: A needle; a life-sized camel cutout, a papier-mâché camel, or a live camel!

Development: The Gospel lesson addresses the theme of discipleship by recalling Jesus' encounter with a rich man who asks what he must do to inherit eternal life. Jesus responds that if he wishes to follow Jesus, he must sell all his possessions and give to the poor, even though he had observed all the commandments from his youth. The outcome is that the rich man leaves disheartened, because he had great wealth.

Tell, with feeling, this superb story about how hard it is for a rich person to enter the realm of God, pointing out how one must put one's whole trust in God as the sole source of security and well-being. Then, as Jesus did, illustrate the major thrust of the story with exaggeration at its best. Jesus said: "It is easier for a camel to go through the eye of a needle than for a rich person to enter the realm of heaven [Mark 10:25]." There has been considerable debate as to what precisely "the eye of a needle" means, but the intent of the image is clearly to show the utter impossibility of getting some huge object through a very small opening. Compare the immensity of a life-sized camel cutout or a papier-mâché camel (or a live camel, if available) with the minuteness of the eye of a common needle to intensify the tight squeeze image. Encourage the children to trust God completely.

Prayer: Dear God, we thank you for camels and needles and for everything that helps us live for you. Amen.

Feelings

Lesson 1: Isaiah 53:7–12
Lesson 2: Hebrews 4:14–16
Gospel: Mark 10:35–45

Theme: We can approach God confidently.
Resource: Finger puppets

Development: The writer of the letter to the Hebrews encourages a group of Christians who were ready to give up their faith because of rising opposition. The second lectionary reading concludes with supportive words: "Let us then with confidence draw near to the throne of grace, that we may receive mercy and find grace to help in time of need [Heb. 4:16]." As Christians, we can go to God with our feelings in confidence and safety and can trust God to give us what we need to deal with them. Jesus, our great high priest, who was tempted but did not sin, is compassionate and sensitive to human need. He believes in us!

Convey this theme to the children today by using finger puppets to represent feelings they have in their own lives. Sock puppets or faces drawn on fingers will work just as well. For each puppet create and offer a brief vignette that describes a feeling, such as sadness (the death of a pet), guilt (having taken something), joy or happiness (receiving a new bike or accomplishing something), disappointment (failing, losing), anger (betrayal by a friend), anticipation (looking forward to vacation), loneliness (best friend moved away). You'll probably want to use only three or four, but try to give a fairly wide range of feelings.

Move on to indicate that no matter how we're feeling we can go to Jesus bravely, without fear, anytime and anywhere, and know that he will understand.

The world of adults and God can be intimidating to children, and they need to be certain that our loving God, through Jesus, is their friend on whom they can depend and with whom they can confidently share their lives.

Prayer: Loving God, thanks for always being my friend. Amen.

PENTECOST 23

Keep On Trying!

Lesson 1: Jeremiah 31:7–9
Lesson 2: Hebrews 5:1–6
Gospel: Mark 10:46–52

Theme: The healing and persistence of Bartimaeus
Resource: A Rubik's Cube

Development: Mark's Gospel this Sunday contains the fabulous story of Jesus' encounter with Bartimaeus, a blind beggar. It celebrates the healing ministry of Jesus and demonstrates the need for and quality of faithful persistence in Christian living.

Internalize this story and tell it in your own words, conveying the two main thoughts. Enable the children to sense the individual personal attention Jesus showed by stopping and healing a social outcast and the firm resolution of Bartimaeus to be heard by Jesus above the din of the rebuking crowd. Emphasize that the key to the healing is found in Jesus' commissioning statement: "Go your way; your faith has made you well [Mark 10:52]."

Illustrate the persistence theme by using a Rubik's Cube. Show how one has to keep on trying different combinations to solve the cube. You don't have to spend a lot of time preparing for this demonstration.

If you have someone in your congregation who is a whiz at this kind of thing, certainly involve that person.

Illustrations on this theme are plentiful (from the universal tying of the shoelaces to riding a bike). It's a good idea to choose activities that the children or others in your Christian community are involved in. Examples in my setting include gymnastics, video games, ballet, horseback riding, hockey, art, singing, and piano. Point out that persistence is not getting one's own way at all costs, but that it is acting faithfully to be the best Christian one can possibly be.

Prayer: Dear God, thank you for all your gifts. Help me to keep on trying for you. Amen.

PENTECOST 24

Reminders

Lesson 1: Deuteronomy 6:1–9
Lesson 2: Hebrews 7:23–28
Gospel: Mark 12:28–34

Theme: The two "great commandments"
Resources: A wrist phylactery and a mezuzah; string; plastic identification bracelet for each child

Development: Both the first lesson and the Gospel record the Shema, the basic principle of the whole Mosaic law and the statement of faith for the Jew that was literally worn on the wrist and forehead. "Hear, O Israel: The Sovereign our God is one God; and you shall love your God with all your heart, and with all your soul, and with all your might. And these words which I command you this day shall be upon your heart; and you shall teach them diligently to your children, and shall talk of them when you sit in your house, and when you walk by the way, and when you lie down, and when you rise. And you shall bind them as a sign upon your hand, and they shall be as frontlets between your eyes. And you shall write them on the doorposts of your house and on your gates [Deut. 6:4–9]."

Show the children a phylactery, which contained the Shema, that was worn on the wrist and a mezuzah, which also contained the Shema, that was fastened to the doorpost of a Jewish home and was touched on entering. Indicate that the phylactery and the mezuzah were reminders of Jewish faith, like we would remind ourselves of something by tying a string around a finger. These "reminders" also signified to others what the Jews believed.

Point out that Jesus, a Jew, quotes the Shema as the first great commandment and then offers the second great commandment: "You shall love your neighbor as yourself [Mark 12:31]." Encourage the children to remember and live by the two great commandments. Give each one a plastic identification bracelet (like the ones used in hospitals) with the second commandment typed on the insert as a reminder.

Prayer: Dear God, I love you with my whole heart and promise to love my neighbor as myself. Amen.

PENTECOST 25

And Now the Offering

Lesson 1: 1 Kings 17:8–16
Lesson 2: Hebrews 9:24–28
Gospel: Mark 12:38–44

Theme: God's gifts are to be shared.

Resources: Two offering plates; two pennies; "lots" of paper currency

Development: All three readings combine to focus on the theme of sharing. The second reading presents Christ as the eternal high priest who has entered the heavenly sanctuary to present the ultimate and perfect sacrifice of himself for sins. The first lesson and the Gospel feature a widow as a major character who demonstrates sharing. The lesson from 1 Kings describes how Elijah provides for the poor widow who was willing to share what little food she had. In the Gospel, Jesus speaks of the widow's faith and her genuine generosity to the church treasury.

Today introduce the children to Jesus' teaching in the Gospel that begins with a strong warning to "beware of the scribes, who like to go about in long robes, and to have salutations in the market places and the best seats in the synagogues and the places of honor at feasts, who devour widows' houses and for a pretense make long prayers [Mark 12:38–40]." Point out the motivation of the scribes, but do have some mercy on them.

Tell the story that follows this warning by using two offering plates. To dramatize the intent of the story, place the paper currency (note that "many rich people put in large sums [Mark 12:41]") in one plate and two coins in the other at the appropriate moment in the story. I have found that there is a tremendous impact when I have let the story literally speak for itself. Encourage the children to recall the widow who gave everything she had and, like her, to commit their whole selves to God.

Prayer: Gracious God, you give us everything. Help us to share your gifts. Amen.

God Was, Is, and Will Be . . . Forever!

Lesson 1: Daniel 7:9–14
Lesson 2: Hebrews 10:11–18
Gospel: Mark 13:24–32

Theme: The enduring nature of God
Resource: Battery-operated toy with a "dead" battery

Development: The lessons from the Old Testament and the Gospel emphasize the enduring nature of God. Daniel's vision observes that "God's dominion is an everlasting dominion, which shall not pass away, and whose realm is one that shall not be destroyed [Dan. 7:14]." The Gospel of Mark records Jesus' statement: "Heaven and earth will pass away, but my words will not pass away [Mark 13:31]."

Clearly, there is an apocalyptic or revelatory character to Jesus' description of the signs of his "second coming," and these should be shared with the children today. Be sure to remind them that the revelation is a "vision," because they tend to understand things quite literally.

The central point to make here is that our God was, is, and will be forever. No matter what happens in heaven or on earth, our God's love will endure to take care of us. To convey this idea, use a battery-operated toy with a dead battery. Express that our God never runs out of energy because our Creator is energy! Affirm with them that we can trust our God to last forever!

Prayer: Dear God, fill me up with your energy so I can live for you. Amen.

Alpha and Omega

Lesson 1: Jeremiah 23:1–6
Lesson 2: Revelation 1:4b-8
Gospel: John 18:33–37

Theme: God is the Alpha and the Omega.
Resource: Greek alphabet symbols alpha and omega

Development: Last Sunday we confirmed the enduring nature of God as everlasting energy. Today we consider another eternal dimension of God by referring to the symbols designated in the second lesson. The Gospel sets the scene for the epistle by noting that Jesus sets his sovereignty in the eternal realm and therefore raises his passion to a level of eternal significance. Jesus said to Pilate: "My sovereignty is not of this world; if my sovereignty were of this world, my servants would fight, that I might not be handed over to the Jews; but my sovereignty is not from the world [John 18:36]." In the epistle, God declares, "I am the Alpha and the Omega . . . who is and who was and who is to come, the Almighty [Rev. 1:8]." Christ the Sovereign is the One who represents and is the Alpha and the Omega.

Show the alpha and omega symbols and explain that they are the first and the last letters of the Greek alphabet, just like the letters *A* and *Z* begin and conclude our alphabet. Make the connection that God is the One who was in the very beginning and the One who will be to the end. Express with confidence, faith, and hope that the God who created us and who sent Jesus to redeem us and the Holy Spirit to inspire us was, is now, and will be forever!

Prayer: Eternal God, we praise you forever and ever. Amen.

INDEX OF SCRIPTURE READINGS (Year B)

Genesis

1:1–5	Epiphany 1
2:18–24	Pentecost 20
3:8–19	Pentecost 21
9:8–17	Lent 1
17:1–10, 15–19	Lent 2

Exodus

20:1–17	Lent 3
24:3–8	Maundy Thursday

Deuteronomy

6:1–9	Pentecost 24
18:15–20	Epiphany 4

1 Samuel

3:1–10	Epiphany 2
16:1–13	Pentecost 2
16:14–23	Pentecost 3

2 Samuel

1:1, 17–27	Pentecost 4
5:1–12	Pentecost 5
6:1–15	Pentecost 6
7:1–17	Pentecost 7

7:8–16	Advent 4
7:18–29	Pentecost 8
11:1–15	Pentecost 9
12:1–14	Pentecost 10
12:15b–24	Pentecost 11
18:1, 5, 9–15	Pentecost 12
18:24–33	Pentecost 13
23:1–7	Pentecost 14

1 Kings

2:1–4, 10–12	Pentecost 15
17:8–16	Pentecost 25

2 Kings

2:1–12a	Epiphany 9
5:1–14	Epiphany 6

2 Chronicles

36:14–23	Lent 4

Job

7:1–7	Epiphany 5
28:20–28	Pentecost 18
42:1–6	Pentecost 19

Proverbs

2:1–8	Pentecost 16
22:1–2, 8–9	Pentecost 17

Isaiah

6:1–8	Trinity Sunday
25:6–9	Easter
40:1–11	Advent 2
43:18–25	Epiphany 7
50:4–9a	Lent 6
52:13—53:12	Good Friday

53:7–12	Pentecost 22
60:1–6	Epiphany
61:1–4, 8–11	Advent 3
61:10—62:3	Christmas 1
62:6–7, 10–12	Christmas Eve/Day
63:16—64:8	Advent 1

Jeremiah

23:1–6	Pentecost 27
31:7–9	Pentecost 23
31:7–14	Christmas 2
31:31–34	Lent 5

Daniel

7:9–14	Pentecost 26

Hosea

2:14–20	Epiphany 8

Joel

2:1–2, 12–17a	Ash Wednesday

Jonah

3:1–5, 10	Epiphany 3

Matthew

2:1–12	Epiphany
6:1–6, 16–21	Ash Wednesday

Mark

1:1–8	Advent 2
1:4–11	Epiphany 1
1:9–15	Lent 1
1:14–20	Epiphany 3
1:21–28	Epiphany 4

1:35–42	Epiphany 2
2:13–22	Lent 3
3:1–17	Trinity Sunday
3:14–21	Lent 4
6:1–15	Pentecost 10
6:24–35	Pentecost 11
6:35, 41–51	Pentecost 12
6:51–58	Pentecost 13
6:55–69	Pentecost 14
10:11–18	Easter 4
12:20–33	Lent 5
15:1–8	Easter 5
15:9–17	Easter 6
15:26–27; 16:4b–15	Pentecost 1
17:11b–19	Easter 7
18:1—19:42	Good Friday
18:33–37	Pentecost 27
20:19–31	Easter 2

Acts

1:15–17, 21–26	Easter 7
2:1–21	Pentecost 1
3:12–19	Easter 3
4:8–12	Easter 4
4:32–35	Easter 2
8:26–40	Easter 5
10:44–48	Easter 6
19:1–7	Epiphany 1

Romans

4:16–25	Lent 2
8:12–17	Trinity Sunday
8:22–27	Pentecost 1
16:25–27	Advent 4

1 Corinthians

1:3–9	Advent 1
1:22–25	Lent 3
6:12–20	Epiphany 2

7:29–31	Epiphany 3
8:1–13	Epiphany 4
9:16–23	Epiphany 5
9:24–27	Epiphany 6
10:16–17	Maundy Thursday
15:1–11	Easter

2 Corinthians

1:18–22	Epiphany 7
3:1–6	Epiphany 8
4:3–6	Epiphany 9
4:5–12	Pentecost 2
4:13—5:1	Pentecost 3
5:6–10, 14–17	Pentecost 4
5:18—6:2	Pentecost 5
5:20b—6:2	Ash Wednesday
8:7–15	Pentecost 6
12:1–10	Pentecost 7

Galatians

4:4–7	Christmas 1

Ephesians

1:1–10	Pentecost 8
1:3–6, 15–18	Christmas 2
2:4–10	Lent 4
2:11–22	Pentecost 9
3:1–12	Epiphany
3:14–21	Pentecost 10
4:1–6	Pentecost 11
4:25—5:2	Pentecost 12
5:15–20	Pentecost 13
6:10–20	Pentecost 15

Philippians

2:5–11	Lent 6

1 Thessalonians

5:16–24   Advent 3

Titus

3:4–7   Christmas Eve/Day

Hebrews

1:1–4; 2:9–11   Pentecost 20
4:1–3, 9–13   Pentecost 21
4:14–16   Pentecost 22
4:14–16; 5:7–9   Good Friday
5:1–6   Pentecost 23
5:7–10   Lent 5
7:23–28   Pentecost 24
9:24–28   Pentecost 25
10:11–18   Pentecost 26

James

1:17–27   Pentecost 16
2:1–5, 8–10, 14–17   Pentecost 17
3:13–18   Pentecost 18
4:13–17; 5:7–11   Pentecost 19

1 Peter

3:18–22   Lent 1

2 Peter

3:8–15a   Advent 2

1 John

1:1—2:2   Easter 2
3:1–7   Easter 3
3:18–24   Easter 4

INDEX OF THEMES

110   INDEX OF THEMES